BECOMING

SILVER GIRL

BECOMING SILVER GIRL

LARISSA FLEURETTE

LIFE RATTLE PRESS • TORONTO, CANADA

MARCH 2015

PUBLISHED IN CANADA BY
LIFE RATTLE PRESS
196 CRAWFORD STREET
TORONTO, ONTARIO M6J 2V6
www.liferattle.ca

Life Rattle Press New Publishers Seriers
ISSN 1713 8981
ISBN 978-1-987936-02-5

Cover Design by Rachelle Ho
Cover Photography by Vanessa Paxton

To the creative spirit that has chosen me to write this book: I dedicate this to you.

The spirit in me acknowledges you.

We have been talking to each other for a while now, and you always knew we'd get this book done somehow, even during the periods some time ago when I was refusing to think or act on what you'd chosen for me to do. I always knew you were the force behind the creation of this book and am eternally grateful to you for choosing me to be the catalyst for the telling of this story.

Thanks. I'll be seeing you.

CONTENTS

Prologue   ix

Chapter 1: Night of the Ceasefire   1

Chapter 2: Not Still Me   7

Chapter 3: Schizophrenia   15

Chapter 4: Daniel   33

Chapter 5: Let It Be Normal   51

Chapter 6: Becoming Silver Girl   57

Chapter 7: Homecoming   65

Chapter 8: Living with Impossibilities   73

Epilogue   81

Acknowledgements   87

About the Author   89

PROLOGUE

WANTING TO BE A WRITER

When I was a child, I would occasionally give up a prayer to the heavens that one day I would be a writer.

The conversations I'd have as a child, desperate, hopeful, and sometimes thankful, would usually revolve around me muttering, "God, I want to write my own book, so please send me a story to write that will be awesome enough to be published... Oh, and please send me some friends who will buy my book, and also, see to bringing around my future husband. Right now. Please. Thanks."

It seemed to me that I wasn't demanding much. I thought that meant God was pleased with me and He would do as I asked, soon enough. All of this made me happy, since though I wasn't seeing right in front of me the story I was requesting, I figured that there was time for it to arrive. I was, after all, all of six years old.

I wanted a story to write so badly, one that would become an actual book that people could take from the library. I was sure that I wouldn't give up, that if I talked to God enough and waited long enough, I would have my own book some day and also even be able to testify to people that God does answer prayers.

During the time that I waited for the wonderful story I'd requested of God to come around, the story that I would instantly recognize as the one I was waiting for, I wrote other stories.

I'd lie on my belly in the library of our house where all my father's books were stacked on shelves, and write in pencil on lined paper of disastrous misfortunes befalling princesses who would need to defend their kingdoms with their wits.

"She writes so much," said my mother to her sister one day as I lay on my stomach on the floor of my father's study, looking up at them, annoyed at their intrusion. "Look. So many pages. She doesn't double-space. It's just one after the other."

My aunt bent down to take a closer look.

"No!" I burst out, covering my paper with both of my hands. "Not done yet!"

"Oh, sorry," said my aunt. Yet I could see that she was still looking!

"Stop!" I said, gathering my papers hurriedly in a messy pile and getting up on my legs. "Looking is cheating," I added, a bit scornfully.

"How is it cheating?" asked my mother.

"Because if you look before it's done you're trying to see what it looks like before anyone else!"

"I'm just curious," said my aunt in an apologetic tone. Then she teased me. "Are you writing love letters to your boyfriend?"

"No! I don't have a boyfriend!" I said. "I'm six."

"Then what are you writing?"

"Stories."

"Ohhhh. What kinds of stories?"

"Some are weird, some are funny."

"Really? What are they about?" she asked, her eyes wide. "Stories of what?"

"Stories of princesses and faraway lands with strange animals," I said with a shrug. "And sometimes, stories of love. That is, *undying* love."

She chuckled.

"What do you know about undying love?" she asked. "What is the definition of undying love? Hmm?"

"I know lots of things!" I jumped around my father's study, gathering my papers and pencil crayons. "What do you mean what is the 'definition'?"

"It is what a word means. What does undying love mean to you?"

"Oh. The definition of undying love is when you love someone until you die and even after you die. That's why it's undying. It also means you would go anywhere with someone so they won't be alone."

"Can I read one of your stories of undying love?"

"No. Because I haven't actually written them. They're still on my list to be written. It's really hard to write a story about undying love," I said in what I thought was my wisest voice. "Right now, the stories are invisible."

She nodded, as if she understood.

"Do you have undying love for anybody?" she asked.

"Not saying," I said, and she raised her eyebrows as if to say, "Why, you cheeky…"

I knew only one thing for sure at that age: that writing and praying soothed me. And I never wanted to forget how to do either of them, even if I was an old lady with Alzheimer's, and if it were ever to happen that I got Alzheimer's, I hoped that someone would reteach me, from scratch, how to write and pray, every single day.

I guessed it would take an extraordinary amount of undying love for someone to do this for me, which was fine with me. What I didn't know was whether I would ever receive it. Stories of undying love were difficult to write, because even though I believed in this kind of love, I had never seen it before.

Prologue

❋   ❋   ❋

I stopped writing at the age of eleven.

I don't remember thinking to myself, "Today is the day I stop writing," but I do remember the day the desire to write no longer washed over me as if it was as essential as breathing.

Were I in possession of a wiser soul, I would have known to keep going in pursuit of writing, because it was a dream, a lovely dream that I thought of as early as the age of five. Were I aware of what it would do to me to stop writing, I'd have plunged forward with conviction, and continued.

Were I a writer in my own eyes, I wouldn't have wanted to stop writing, because who has the audacity to allow their vocation to slip through their fingers? It is not easily done. You don't just glance at the realization that you were meant to be a writer, or a singer, or a plumber, or a teacher, or an accountant, say, "Nice to meet you; goodbye, so long" and walk away. I don't think that's how it works. Just a glance at some part of the reason that you exist, that you are here, should be enough to silence you in awe, and cause you to struggle to keep your vocation from slipping away.

I saw myself not as a writer, only a girl who wanted to write. I wanted to create a story from scratch and have it go from there to wherever I wanted it to go. I wrote story after story on blank paper in pencil while sprawled on my belly on the floor of my father's study at home. I wouldn't dare call myself a writer, however. I wouldn't. A writer was someone who knew how to write and didn't have to spend hours wondering what to put down on paper. They just knew where the story was to go. They were dedicated to the craft. They were good at what they did.

Writing was a fun thing to do, making up characters and what they looked like and even what their favourite colour was, but it was also a serious thing. I felt whenever I wrote that I was somehow writing for the world, and this, however much an imaginary mission given to me by myself, filled me with a sense of deep pride and purpose.

What it never did was give me confidence. I always felt that the things I wrote were lacking in importance, and that even though now my piece of paper was filled with words, it may as well have been blank, for all anyone cared. It may as well have never been written, because no one would read it. And it may as well have never been thought of, for all the good it did me. I should have, I often felt, decided to spend my time on something else that would possibly be more worthwhile.

I stopped writing at the age of eleven. Everything seemed so pointless in that moment when I chose not to put pen to paper, and not writing was not going to make things any worse.

The sudden stop to writing in my life was jarring. I didn't know what to do with myself, I think. I didn't know that not writing was making me feel irritable, depressed, hopeless. Or had I felt all those things before I stopped? Are these feelings what caused me to stop? What came first?

Where did the insanity originate?

However, I still believe that nothing—not even the act of giving up on writing—made me feel as wretched as the screaming evil spirits that came to visit me one night when I was trying to fall asleep at the age of eleven.

CHAPTER 1

NIGHT OF THE CEASEFIRE

The night of the ceasefire, as I call it when I talk to myself about it, was the night a miracle happened.

I've never told anyone about it before, as I don't know if they'd agree with how or what makes that event a miracle and besides, I don't need anyone else to validate to me that it actually was. I know it was. I don't know how to describe how I know. I just *know*.

The night of the ceasefire happened a couple of weeks before my fifteenth birthday.

That particular night, I stared at myself in the mirror at around two in the morning. I stared at my small heaving chest and pale skin and haunted eyes spilling tears in a small puddle on the counter. I forgot all the rules of praying and found myself asking God for His help. No words. No knees on the ground. No hands clasped together. No head bowed. I didn't speak. I just felt. I warred internally with myself on reaching out to God, a God who I didn't believe, for years, existed.

I'd just ripped up my journal where I'd documented the past year of my life, damaged the journal beyond recognition. Then I tore the broken pages into pieces that fluttered to the floor of my father's study. I tore it into pieces because I couldn't bear the thought of the past year, which, whenever I thought about it, revolted me.

Besides how I felt about it, I somehow hoped, I think, that by tearing up my journal and making the words in it disappear, I'd make the events that took place, that had been documented in that journal, disappear as well.

After tearing it up, I didn't feel any different. I wasn't soothed. And the events that had taken place the year before had still happened. Ripping up the journal did not mean that these things no longer happened. They still lingered there, in the past.

Nothing had actually happened in the past year. The truth was, on the surface nothing had happened, but on the inside, I was suffering for the past year, as I had suffered since I was eleven, but the suffering had increased in a way I didn't know was possible. I thought nothing could feel as bad as it did at the age of eleven. I was wrong.

I stared at my face in the mirror and all the attempts I had made to make things better seemed to rise up before me and gloat at me. They seemed to taunt me. The attempts to be strong hadn't worked, and because of that, I was a failure. I was inadequate.

My eyes seemed to have this crazy, haunted look in them. They were like a shark's eyes, menacing, ready to kill as they looked at my pale face. Tears leaked out. My breathing was ragged. My hair was dry and falling out.

I needed help and I thought I knew someone who would possibly be able to help me in a way that no one else could. I didn't move. I was afraid to ask for help.

I suppose I didn't speak mostly because I was so afraid to speak to God. I was so miserable. I hadn't spoken to Him in so long. I even told people I didn't believe in Him. What gave me the license to speak to Him, after denying Him?

Try. Speak in the silence without words and see if anyone responds.

Asking for help without actually asking seemed like a foreign thing to do. But then, I somehow felt that this simple act of sitting still in the silence had reached God somehow.

He heard every word in my heart. He didn't need

my words to tell him what the heck was going on. He already knew. I didn't need the bells and whistles of prayer to qualify me as a person worthy of speaking to God. It was only until I'd broken the rules of prayer that I started to truly pray. All I had done and felt and thought and hoped and refused to pray for, He knew. He knew how I felt when I didn't know.

I saw in the mirror all the haunting in my eyes deflate, as if what haunted me realized it did not have power any longer. The strain on my shoulders until then had felt so heavy, but in this moment, wasn't quite so raw. I felt I didn't need to think anymore about trying to end my life. I slipped off the counter in the bathroom, feeling light, and headed to bed.

Something strange was happening in my body. With every step I took, I felt stronger, as if an anchor I'd been pulling around that had been tied to my ankles had suddenly been cut loose and now I was free. I felt sure that every word I'd ever said to God had been heard, and I'd reached out to Him after years of wandering about in the dark on my own, and had without speaking a word. I'd witnessed Him coming back to get me from my despair and we'd been reunited.

I didn't know how I knew this. I just believed that God had saved me, for no reason, other than that He could, and He'd chosen to.

I got into bed and more tears came. I didn't feel alone anymore. I'd just been reunited with my friend, my dear God. I realized then that praying didn't necessarily mean saying anything to God aloud, and all the best prayers I'd ever prayed didn't present themselves to God in words, but in silences.

I had stopped praying, both with and without words, and refused God, but the moment I decided to come back to Him, He'd scooped me up from the wretchedness and now I felt myself floating as if in Heaven, bathed in contentment, as if the whole world had called a ceasefire just to allow me to sleep through the night. It was a miracle.

I slept in utter peace and didn't awake once, in probably the first night of uninterrupted sleep I'd had since the night when I was eleven, when I first heard the voices.

CHAPTER 2

NOT STILL ME

I stand in the doorway, waiting and taking in the vibrant colours of the toys sitting silently on the shelves, the soothing tan of the walls, and the huge framed pictures of smiling, laughing children. The office smells faintly like freshly squeezed lemons. I glimpse a picture of a smiling girl sitting on the desk as I sit down in the chair he gestures to with an open palm. The girl has big green eyes. A toothy smile. Chocolate brown hair. A huge sunflower is nestled between her open palms, held out as an offering to the person behind the camera.

I am met inevitably with the face of Dr. Quinn. Observing me with keen eyes, both hands folded in his lap, he sits on a padded chair, legs crossed, a dark purple tie around his neck. My insides squirm when I meet his bright eyes. I look into his lined, gentle face and feel ashamed that this nice man has to see me like this, ragged and undone, unkempt and coming loose like a badly tied knot. I feel as if something bad is about to happen—something unpredictable and out of my control.

"Hello, Larissa," Dr. Quinn says calmly. His voice startles me. "Please, have a seat over there."

He gazes at me, seemingly without hurry. I try to see myself through his eyes. My hands grip the arms of the cushioned chair I have sunk into, squeezing as if I'm steeling myself against some unknown pain. I try to remember that he doesn't want to hurt me. I can *see* that he doesn't, but my mind is in chaos, panic, despair, and most of all, grief, which is a strange emotion to have when one has not a thing to grieve about.

Dr. Quinn speaks to me slowly. He's going to ask me some questions, he says.

I concentrate on the picture of the smiling girl on his desk, look into the girl's wide grin, and try to infuse myself with her happiness, with the sunshine showering her. I imagine myself smiling as she is smiling. It seems like a foreign thing for my lips to do.

"So, you are in grade eleven at St. Marcellinus. Your birthday was in July... You're sixteen. Okay. How are you doing in school?" Dr. Quinn asks.

What an absolutely ordinary question. It surprises me. Why does he want to know? What is he going to do to me if I don't answer honestly? What will the consequences be?

"I don't know." My voice comes out softer than I've ever heard it. "I don't go to school anymore."

"Why is that, Larissa?" He seems to be searching for something in my eyes, but not insistently, but gently, like he knows he'll find it if he doesn't hurry. He's investigating me, I think.

There is nothing to fear from this man, I realize... Nothing at all.

"I'm scared." I blurt it out as if admitting to something shameful.

"Why are you scared? Is it the teachers, the students, the work?" He looks concerned, as if this truly troubles him. I don't understand why it would, but I don't have time to think of that now. I have to think of the answer to his question, a question I can't quite remember right now. How strange. After a moment, he repeats the question.

"I just—I can't... I can't make decisions very well. I don't feel so good."

"Hmmm..." A few lines appear between his eyebrows. *Please*, I say in my mind to whoever may be able to help me, *make me normal again. God? Please make me normal again.*

"What about your friends?" asks Dr. Quinn.

"Don't you want to see them?"

"I don't want them... to see me... like *this*."

I have voiced my greatest fear—that those I so cherish would be disgusted by my relentless routine of sleeping, eating, crying. I resolved a while ago not to let them ever find this out about me.

He nods slowly, as if he agrees with me, or if something has registered suddenly in his mind. Then he continues questioning me. How do I feel about school? Am I sleeping well at night? How is my appetite? Why don't I think I have one? So. I'm not eating? At all? And sleeping. You're in bed, all night and all day?

I can barely keep up with his questions. I try to seem fine. I try to relax more, breathe, and meet his eyes. My shoulders are hunched up to my ears. *Help me, God. Help me, please.*

I look at Dr. Quinn's shiny black shoes, at the neat knot he has made with his shoelaces. I try to think of the picture of the girl with the sunflower because it made me feel better before, but I can't quite grasp the picture in my mind. I feel dizzy, like my mind has been whirling for hours.

"Are you afraid to be in the room right now, Larissa?" Dr. Quinn asks then.

"No," I lie. I don't want him to know how shivery and vulnerable I am, helpless and lost. He may hurt me if he knows.

"Are you afraid to be in the room right now, Larissa?" he repeats. His voice, for the first time, sounds stern. I glance up from his shoes to his face. He looks like he's seeing an injured animal. It's the look of someone who has seen an injured animal too many times.

"A little," I whisper.

"Why?" His eyes are narrowed as he watches me.

"I don't know."

"Do you feel like hurting yourself?"

"No."

"What are you thinking about right now?"

"I want to go to sleep."

A pause. He seems to be waiting for me to say more. I don't.

"Your mom is outside in the waiting area, isn't she?" he asks.

"Yes."

"Larissa, it could be a lot of things... but why don't we call your mother in and I can talk to you both at the same time? Wait here, please." He gets up and walks briskly towards the closed door, opens it and leaves the office with me inside with the toys and pictures of smiling people. I wonder how he can be in possession of so much more energy than me, a kid probably more than thirty years his junior. I don't want to look at the picture of the girl with the sunflower. I am ashamed to realize I am jealous of her happiness.

When Dr. Quinn comes back, my mother is with him. She looks like she's about to cry. He gestures for her to sit down in a chair next to me. She does, far slower than I've ever seen her move. I feel like giving her a hug, but I don't. I'm afraid that if I do, I will give her false hope that everything is okay, and if it's not, that it will get better. I can't let her carry on believing a lie. I love her too much to let her continue believing that I'm still here... still me. I'm not still me. As much as I want to be me, for her, and for the family, I can't. I'm dead and gone.

"It could be a lot of things," Dr. Quinn says again, looking at me when he speaks. "I think it's best we get her checked into a hospital immediately."

A *hospital*?!

"I've been thinking about this for a while now. A few years ago, Larissa was an A student, performing above average and was considered for the gifted program at her school. She had many friends and was a happy child. Now, she's not very responsive, she isn't functioning normally, she's not eating, sleeps too much, and I don't know what it is. What we have here is a deterioration of a model student... So, I think it's best they did a full assessment at the hospital. Just to make sure she's okay."

I turn my head and look at my mother's stunned face. I almost reach out my hand to touch her on her shoulder, make her feel better. But I don't. I feel my eyes watering.

"Where would she go?" Mama asks in a petrified voice.

"There's no adolescent unit in Mississauga," says Dr. Quinn, "so she would go to the nearest one, in Brampton. I will put in a referral today so the hospital staff can put her on the waitlist for an in-patient bed. Hopefully she won't have to wait too long for one to become available."

Silence.

"What are you thinking, Larissa?" says Dr. Quinn. "You need to go to the hospital."

They wait for me to answer. I try to think of what to say, but the words aren't coming easily.

"I don't think that's a good idea," I finally get out.

"Why not, Larissa?" Dr. Quinn asks calmly.

"I don't need to go; I'm fine..."

"Larissa," Dr. Quinn says in his soothing way. "You haven't been to school in weeks. You can barely get out of bed. You're afraid to be out in public. You don't look me in the eye when I talk to you. Paranoia, depression, anxiety... these are not good signs. I want you to get better, Larissa. They can help you at the hospital. They will run tests to make sure everything is working physiologically, perform a CAT scan and an MRI. That's what I'm most interested in. She will also undergo other tests with a psychologist there."

"What kind of tests?" asks my mother.

"I don't want to go," I say quietly. They both look at me.

"I don't want to get better," I say. "I want to go to sleep."

Dr. Quinn nods at Mama.

"We'll be in touch," he says gently.

Mama nods and gets up. I do too, thinking I'm a horrible person for making this happen. Still, even more than self-loathing, I feel afraid, so afraid, almost as if I'm wandering lost on the other side of the world, alone, searching for reason and logic in a strange corner of the planet where no reason or logic exists.

CHAPTER 3

SCHIZOPHRENIA

Just as when Dr. Quinn sentenced me to this hospital last week, I am terrified.

There is no turning back from this once I am admitted. This is the turning point in my maniacal downhill deterioration from a "model student" into a member of an even lower species of human—the mentally ill.

They've given me a hospital band that says my name, the hospital name, and that I'm allergic to penicillin. I twirl it around my wrist as we wait in emergency, Mama and I.

Everyone from now on will see in my hospital file that I was admitted to this hospital for being a mental person, even though in the future there's a possibility that I will no longer be mental.

This act of being admitted will follow me around for the rest of my life. It will be written there until I die, that I, Mei-Hui Larissa Fleurette Ho, was, and possibly still am, *mental*.

I think of what will happen if I witness someone doing an injustice to someone else. What will happen if I witness a murder and the police call me in to their police station later to identify the murderer? Somehow, someone will discover that I'm simply not a credible witness, that I'm crazy, that they can't trust me. They won't take my testimony seriously. The murderer will get away because they can't say that I have properly identified the correct man or woman!

Imagine that. Now I'm going to be in this mental health unit, which is a whole other world where they've taken me to be closer to happiness and good health... It's also one step closer to being confirmed "crazy."

I can't go. I can't go.

Dr. Quinn said they want to make sure I'm okay. People are worried because I'm horribly depressed and suffering like how people do when they've just lost a relative or had their hearts broken, and for absolutely no reason.

Nothing *happened* to me. Except for the fact that I was happy, a happy and carefree child, nothing happened to me. No one I loved died. No one left me, abandoned me, hurt me, defiled me. I was happy until one day, I woke up and wasn't.

That's it.

It is a huge source of shame for me to not have a reason to be depressed and be depressed regardless. It makes me think there is no meaning to my depression, that maybe I just made it up, or am too weak to enjoy life like any normal person would be able to.

I feel hot and sweaty in my jeans and sweater as I walk beside Mama with my backpack full of clothes and toiletries hanging over my right shoulder from the emergency unit.

The mental health unit is in the dark and depressing basement. As soon as we step out of the elevator, my stomach takes a dive and I feel like running back to the elevator and insisting that Mama take me home. It is a dark dungeon with few lights and it smells strange, like a combination of oldness and cleanliness.

Walking towards us is a tall, gaunt man wearing a hospital gown. His walk is slow and has a floating kind of feel to it, as if he's not actually feeling the ground that his socked feet are touching. His skin is pale, like he hasn't been in the sunlight for a long time.

He turns into the adult mental health unit and Mama propels me forward to the adolescent unit.

Here we are.

"I'm Julia," says the nurse behind the front desk when we walk in. "You must be Larissa. You're her mom?"

"Yes," says Mama.

"Follow me, ladies."

Julia walks us to an office and asks Mama and I to be seated at the desk.

"I need to grab your file, Larissa, so please wait here for a moment."

She leaves Mama and me alone.

"Ma," I say to her as soon as we are alone in Julia's office, "I'll try to get better by myself, you know. I don't really need to be here."

"You do! You do!" she insists. I fall silent, startled by her conviction. I don't know what to do.

One day, the stars are going to align to give me strength and peace to live my life again.

Until that day comes, why should we worry about what's happening in between? What can we do? I've tried everything, absolutely everything, to help myself get better so that the family doesn't have to suffer through me anymore. Nothing is going to work. Nothing is going to change, not even stuffing me in this hospital.

Julia returns with my file, sits down and starts to direct questions at Mama.

What's Larissa's date of birth? What are her allergies? How many other children do you have? Does Larissa get along with her siblings? Was your pregnancy with Larissa a normal pregnancy? Was there any unusual circumstance surrounding the pregnancy? Was there anything unusual about Larissa's intellectual development throughout her childhood?

I can't keep track of all her questions. There are too many.

Finally, she says, "Mrs. Ho, she'll be okay with us. I think we're all done here, Larissa. I just need a few moments alone with your mom."

She gestures for me to leave the office and sit outside on a chair.

For some reason, I find I don't really care that I'm here, not as much as I cared this morning. Let them do what they want with me. I don't care what happens in the outside world anymore. I'm in this other world, in the mental health unit, where it's understood that I'm crazy. I no longer need to try to pretend I'm fine. It's better this way. Pretending just takes up too much of my energy.

❋ ❋ ❋

The unit is small, with only enough room for ten beds, a nursing station, a shower, a meeting room, a schoolroom and the psychiatrists' offices.

I share a room with a girl about my age. Her

name is Daniella. She has short chestnut hair, pale skin and a tired face.

After my mother has left me alone with my backpack of clothes and toiletries, Daniella and I sit on our two parallel beds, facing each other. She studies me. I look down without meaning to, stare without seeing my feet. Something inside me doesn't feel right, but what else is new these days?

"What are you on?" is the first thing Daniella says to me. I look up at her in surprise.

"What am I on?" I say.

"Medication." Her eyes are dull. They have no life in them, almost like the life has been seeped out of them by a black hole or something.

"Oh. Nothing yet," I say.

"Your psychiatrist never put you on anything?" she asks. Her voice is raspy as if she has a cold.

"I'd only been seeing him for two months before he referred me here."

She is on antidepressants and antipsychotics, as well as birth control pills, and the patch, which is supposed to help her quit smoking.

I try not to show my astonishment. How can anyone be medicated with so many different things?

"Oh," I say, hoping that this response will suffice. "How old are you?"

"Seventeen. You?"

"Sixteen."

"I'm bipolar. What are you?"

"I don't know. Hopefully not anything," I respond.

She nods. "Hopefully."

She is a little strange, but I like her.

"It really sucks to have something," she says. "I've been in three different hospitals in the past two years. I've been on like, twenty different combinations of medications... I fucking hate it."

I nod as if I understand. What a nightmare. I feel as if I'm going to cry. That wouldn't help her at all.

There is a picture of a boy in a graduation cape framed on her dresser. I feel I should ask her about him, talk about something else, but in truth, I don't feel like talking about anything. All I want to do is sleep, even though I've slept more than ten hours since I went to bed last night.

All the hope I felt after I thought I reconnected with God the week after my fifteenth birthday has wandered off, and the memory of that night no longer brings me comfort but apprehension that maybe I just imagined that God and I had reunited. Maybe it was simply a delusion.

Yet sometimes when I lie in bed as I try to sleep, I remember that night and don't simply feel some comfort, but instead, something more. It's the happiest of feelings, as if rejoicing angels have come to visit me in encouragement, and they're happy that I'm still trying. They whisper to me not to give up, even though I feel like caving in so, so badly.

I wonder if God is rooting for me somehow, wanting me to win against this thing. He's probably the one who sent those angels!

God wants me to win. I feel buoyed up by the thought, the thought of God watching me and cheering me on in my battle against this silly damned hopelessness that gnaws at me. However silly this hopelessness is, I guess it must have some boldness, to be hurting me like this in front of God.

Let it try to overcome me. Everyone knows you can't lose when God is on your side.

I realize my legs are swinging back and forth as they dangle down.

Daniella stares at me.

"Daniella, do you think you're… you know, going to get better?" She stares at me with her vacant eyes. I struggle to get my words out. "Are you hopeful about getting better? One day?"

"I don't know," she says. "I don't think so. Maybe if they find the right combination of medications. I don't know how or when they're going to do it… It's taking fucking forever."

A knock on the door interrupts her. A man's voice calls to us from outside the room.

"Is Larissa in there? It's Dr. Chakraborty. I'd

like a few words."

I jump up and open the door, where a tired-looking man is waiting. I close the door behind me and follow him out the unit and down the hallway, past the adult unit.

He doesn't speak until we get to his office.

"Larissa," he says. "Have a seat. Make yourself comfortable." He sits. I sit across from him, taking in his notepad and clipboard and his boxy glasses.

"Dr. Quinn referred you to us. He's concerned about you."

Dr. Chakraborty looks at me, waiting for me to speak. I wait too.

No. I have nothing to say.

"I'm going to ask you a few questions," he continues. "Is that okay? So, Larissa, Larissa, Larissa… Here we are. How are you feeling?"

"Good," I say, afraid to say anything else. I never tell strangers what I'm actually feeling. Does anyone actually expect to hear the truth after asking that question?

"Do you sometimes have strange thoughts?" the doctor asks.

"No." As soon as I say this, I doubt that's the truth.

"Have you ever experienced hallucinations?"

"Yeah…"

"What were they like?"

"They were voices that were not really there." I understand, as I say this, that it isn't my fault that I heard voices that weren't really there, yet somehow I feel guilty.

"I see. What did they say to you?" He doesn't look surprised.

"They screamed at me. I couldn't understand what they were saying."

"Hmmm. Do you feel anxious a lot?"

"Yes."

"Why?"

"I don't know."

"I see. Do you have problems making decisions or with your memory?"

"Yes." I feel like I'm hurrying to keep up. I don't know why the questions are coming so fast.

"Your parents have been concerned about you because you are sleeping too much and crying at night. Is this true?"

"Yeah."

"You're moody. You don't go out with your friends anymore. You're often angry and don't do the things you liked to do when you were younger, such as play the piano, read or watch movies."

"I guess." I don't like that he knows so much about me. All of it seems like material he could use to hurt me.

"Larissa, I'm sorry to tell you this but I think—in

24

fact, I'm fairly certain—you have schizophrenia."

"Schizo... Schizo...phrenia?" I stumble over the word.

He nods. I stare at him, dumb. I feel as if he's punched me in the stomach. Does this mean I'm actually crazy? Sick? Will I ever live again? Oh my God. Dear God.

He taps his foot and looks down at his notes. Wow. Schizophrenia. Just like that? How can he diagnose me within five minutes?

"How do you *know*?" I ask, my voice coming out in a plea for him to take back what he said.

"Larissa, I've seen many patients and treated many of them with the same ailments as you. I'm fairly certain that you are suffering from schizophrenic symptoms."

"Really? But... But—I can't be—schizophrenic."

"What do you mean, Larissa? You confirmed to me, just a few moments ago, that you are suffering from hallucinations, delusions, paranoia and depression. Am I right?"

"Yeah," I say.

"Well. How do you feel about this diagnosis?" he asks, looking from me to his clipboard.

"I don't get it," I say. I can't tell him that my thoughts have become chaotic in the last few moments, as soon as he mentioned the word "schizophrenia."

I don't feel like myself anymore. Where is God? I try to remember the night of the ceasefire to bring myself some immediate comfort, but I can't think of that night with the s-word rolling around in my brain.

"I'm sorry, Larissa. Please be patient and don't panic. I will speak to you in the morning with your parents," he says. "They are coming for an appointment with me tomorrow."

I watch him get up.

Please don't leave, I feel like saying. I want him to take back what he said about being schizophrenic, or ask me some more questions so that he can change his mind and the diagnosis.

"Are you sure about this diagnosis?" I ask him, trying to elevate my voice and sound more forceful and confident. I can't; I'm in a panic. "You're sure?"

"Yes," he says and that's all he will say before he opens the door and gestures for me to leave.

I'm not the insane one in this room, you are, I say to him silently as I take my leave and return down the hall to the room I share with Daniella.

It is four in the afternoon. I get in bed and try to digest the diagnosis. I can't. The thought of it is shocking. I try to breathe. What would a good big sister of Rachelle, Stephanie, Mathias and Elizabeth do? What would I have done, if this were ten years ago? Am I going to panic or am I going to think clearly?

What would the siblings want me to do? What would make my parents proud?

Dr. Chakraborty is trying to hurt me. He doesn't care.

But he's the doctor here. Not me. He knows what he's talking about.

I always have suspected that there is something wrong with me, for the past three years. I didn't know at the age of eleven that hearing the voices meant that I was crazy. I thought them to be real, thought they were evil spirits. And now, at age sixteen, I have to admit that there is something deeper than a foggy mind happening to me. There are times I'm terribly depressed. I am anxious a lot. I think strange thoughts.

But *schizophrenia*? What is it? How did I get it?

When I can't think anymore, I fall asleep as my iPod plays with my ear buds in my ears. I fall asleep listening to "Bed of Roses" by Bon Jovi. I fall asleep wanting it to be ten years ago, when I was okay, happy, excited, and full of life.

I fall asleep thinking of myself running around the house screaming each equation in the multiplication chart to help me remember my multiplication, pushing my baby brother on the swing in the park near our house, singing songs that I made up to pass the time until I became a real singer. Where did I go? Where is the Larissa who once existed?

And if God can make miracles happen, why hasn't He done it yet? Why can't He heal me of this schizophrenia, whatever it is?

❋ ❋ ❋

Someone shakes me and I awake with a start.

"Larissa," says a voice.

I open my eyes. The voice belongs to a red-haired nurse with a sour face. I turn away so I don't have to see the sourness in her expression.

"Dr. Chakraborty prescribed this medication for you. You can't go to bed without taking it tonight."

"What is it?" I ask drowsily.

"An antipsychotic called Risperidone."

"I don't want to take it."

"Dr. Chakraborty said you are to take it."

"I don't want to."

But I do, because while I'm a patient here, I will do as the doctor says.

It's a little white pill that's so soft I can crush it into powder just by squeezing it gently between my fingers. When I put it on my tongue, it dissolves before I sip the remainder of my apple juice that was sitting on my dresser to help it go down.

"Thank you," says the nurse. "Now you may go to sleep."

I lie back down and try to do that, but I cry instead. When Daniella comes in to sleep in her bed, she hears me crying, but she doesn't say anything. I stifle my tears after she turns out the lights, not wanting to bother her. I think of the people at school. What did they learn today? What things did they talk about at lunch? Did they notice my absence?

I'm not sure when I fall asleep. But when I wake up next, it is four-thirty in the morning. A slit in the curtain covering the window beside my bed shines through with moonlight, or perhaps with the light from a streetlamp.

My head feels so chaotic. I feel as if a million thoughts are fighting their way to the front of my brain, trying to get some attention, but none of them are allowing each other to get through, and so they're just whirling around beneath the surface of consciousness, so that I don't know what I'm supposed to be thinking. I feel confused, strange, stretched beyond the limit. This feeling is nothing new. I often feel it during the day as well. But it rarely wakes me up at night. My hair is damp with sweat and tears. I am cold.

The wind outside is howling. I feel as if it's angry at me. It could be God, trying to send me a message, trying to say He's angry at me. The wind seems to be in the room itself, seems to be in the very cold air that surrounds my body and my uncovered head. I pull the sheets so that my head is submerged, but the air seems still to be very alive, moving around, and making whispery noises.

I hear it then, beneath the wind in the small room. It's near to me. Footsteps.

Is the nurse coming? Can she hear the wind in the room? Then I realize it's not coming from outside. The footsteps are in the room. They're walking back and forth by the foot of my bed, slowly and incessantly. I strain to hear more clearly.

Is it there? Do I really hear it?

As I try to confirm to myself that there is someone in the room walking there in front of me, a voice starts warbling gibberish.

It shouts. Voices chime in, yelling incomprehensibly, mingling together in a confusing mesh, as if trying to drown each other out. They sound furious. They are angry enough to hurt me if they wanted.

I shut my eyes tight and try to move but I can't move, I can't breathe, I can't make a sound.

Daniella snores in her bed a few feet away from me, and I realize that she is real... The voices aren't, or she wouldn't still be sleeping throughout their screaming, would she?

I throw the hospital linens back and run past the invisible being walking back and forth in front of my bed, past Daniella's, out the door, to the nursing station. I run in my bare feet, my hands outstretched in front of me. I feel as if I am not in control of my own body, and that I may do something unexpected, like collapse in a heap on the floor.

A woman looks up from her computer, startled, when I barge in from my room, stifling screams.

"Larissa?! Is everything okay?"

Rising quickly from her chair, the nurse holds her arms out towards me as if to catch me if I should fall. I don't fall, though. I stand before her, hysterical, my voice rising by the second.

"There were voices in my room! They were trying to tell me something!"

She looks even more startled. "Larissa! There's no one there..."

"I know, but I could hear them. And there were footsteps walking in front of my bed. I couldn't even move. I couldn't even move! I couldn't even move! Oh my God!"

"Larissa," she says soothingly. "Don't worry. There's no one there. Okay? Larissa? Larissa, listen to me." Her voice is stern now. "Go back to bed. There's no one there."

I return to my room. I look at the foot of my bed to see the being that was walking.

There's no one there.

I am afraid that the voices will wake me up if I try to sleep again, so I stay awake until I hear the other patients stir and start to come out of their rooms.

How many more times do I have to hear the voices? When will they leave me alone? I try to pray as I hear patients and nurses speaking outside the door, the breakfast trays coming in from the kitchens, and people taking their morning showers. I try to pray because I feel so alone and I know that right now God is the only person I can talk to. But as I try to formulate the words to send to him, all I get is a block in my mind and an empty feeling in my heart, as if God has left and doesn't think I'm worth coming back to.

CHAPTER 4

DANIEL

I struggle to calm my mind and get out of bed at around eight. It feels as if something is forcibly holding me down to the bed and giving my brain matter a shake so that the contents inside are all jumbled. All I want to do is sleep and never wake again.

"Are you coming to group?" asks Daniella in the bed beside me. There are dark circles under her eyes. She looks so much older than she actually is.

I wonder what I look like. Probably like shit. If there was a way, I would change things, so that the people who work hard to be alive and lead a normal life would get what they wanted.

Unfortunately, there's no way of guaranteeing that one who works for what they want will get it,

I guess. Sometimes we aren't promised happiness. And who are we to complain? Do we even deserve happiness?

"I am coming to group. The nurse who admitted me said it's obligatory," I say. "Is it really?"

Daniella nods.

I climb out of bed and walk in my bare feet to the dining area. More than ten teenagers are sitting around a tray on the table where sample-sized peanut butter and jam portions are scattered. Everyone is eating toasted bread and drinking orange juice or milk.

I'm not hungry so I walk to the adjoining room, where a TV sits, and the other nurses are waiting.

I wait for group to begin.

After the other patients join us, group begins. It seems that group consists of each patient introducing themselves and saying what their goal was for the day before and what their goal is for today.

When my turn comes to speak, I say, "I'm Larissa..."

Before I can continue by saying what my goal for today is, a teenage guy about my age across the room blurts out, "Why are you here? God, you look so normal!"

"I'd appreciate you giving Larissa the space to say what her goal is," says the nurse who is taking attendance and writing down what everyone's goals are. "We don't interrupt each other during group."

"Sorry," he says, and I continue.

"My goal is to talk to my psychiatrist today about discharge."

"You can't be discharged. You just got here," says the guy.

"Excuse me, Paul. It's Larissa's turn, not your turn," says the nurse.

"Sorry," he says. His head droops on his shoulders, looking too big for the rest of his body.

"So you want to ask Dr. Chakraborty about discharge?"

"Yes."

She nods. I can tell my goal for this day isn't going to work out.

After group, it's time to go to the schoolroom to catch up on the homework that schools have sent each of us in order to keep up with the rest of our peers who are still out there in the real world.

All I want to do is write poetry. Although the poetry I write is bad, it keeps away all the weird and random things that cycle through my mind during the day. I try to list some of the books I want to read before I die. *Jane Eyre* tops the list, followed by *Les Miserables* and *The Catcher in the Rye*.

I look around the room and realize there is a bookshelf behind my chair. I turn around, select a tattered and torn copy of *The Great Gatsby*, and begin to read for the next two hours.

I don't hear Mr. Wolsley, the school teacher, saying my name quietly at the front of the room until the other patients start to help him.

"Larissa! Larissa!"

I look up.

Mr. Wolsley motions for me to go to the door, so I close my book and walk over, wondering if my mother is here to see me.

It is not my mother. It is a man. He is wearing a button-down shirt and khaki pants and has long blond hair tied up in a ponytail.

Looking at him, I don't feel afraid. Instead, I feel a different reaction from the one I had to Dr. Chakraborty, whose tired appearance made me feel even more enervated than before.

This man, for whatever reason—maybe it is the earnest look of open honesty on his face—makes me feel eager to think about ways to get myself better, which I haven't done in the few weeks leading up to the hospital.

Perhaps I can get better so that I can impress him with my ability to bounce back from my slight depression! Maybe I can show him that I'm actually a resilient soul, capable of recovery without him! And I do want to impress him.

I want to get better! I will get better! I must triumph!

As I stare at him, I notice his ponytail again. Interesting.

He nods at me, then turns and walks away from me. I follow him, looking at his ponytail. This man is a rebel, I conclude to myself, and that makes him similar to me.

When we get to his little office, I sit down on a wooden chair and watch the man sit down on the wheelie chair.

"I'm Dr. Daniel Gabrielson, I'm a psychologist, and I'm here to do some tests with you."

"What kinds of tests?" I ask.

Instead of answering, he pulls out a clipboard. I watch his eyes go back and forth quickly across the clipboard and realize he's skimming information about me. What does it say about me that I don't know?

I feel a little embarrassed. Does he now know things about me that reveal how stupid and hateful I am?

He flips the page over the top of the clipboard and continues reading on the second page. I sit as still as I can and notice that I am holding my breath. I let it out in a loud sigh. He still doesn't look up.

I want to know what is written about me on the paper.

I can just imagine what it says: "Girl, sixteen, very psycho. Must be taken to another facility immediately for twenty-four-hour surveillance. Should not be allowed to mingle with normal people ever again..."

I notice that Dr. Gabrielson is staring at me. I feel my stomach churning.

"What are you thinking about?"

His tone confuses me. It's not like a psychologist type of voice. It sounds so much like a friend asking me what's up. It's soothing, not scary.

"Nothing," I say.

He looks back down at his clipboard. I sense I have given the wrong answer, and that he really wanted to know the true answer.

"Does it say I'm schizophrenic?" I ask.

He looks up. "Why do you ask?" he says.

"That's what Dr. Chakraborty says I am," I say, trying to sound as if I don't really care what I am one way or another.

My straight back and my alert eyes are a sham, a sham to cover up how ill I feel, mentally, emotionally and physically. All of it is to make him think I'm much more well than I actually am. Why am I going through this charade, I wonder? Is it because I want him to discharge me?

He looks thoughtful.

"Dr. Chakraborty believes you are schizophrenic," he agrees.

"Yeah! He didn't even talk to me for more than

five minutes before he said that!"

"But I don't."

"You don't?" I ask. "But Dr. Chakraborty... I mean, he's a psychiatrist and you're a psychologist, so he's more qualified, right? Dr. Gabrielson?"

He puts the clipboard gently on the table between us, and leans back in his wheelie chair. I resist the urge to look at the clipboard and read what it says upside down.

"First of all, call me Daniel."

I stare at him.

"Second of all, Dr. Chakraborty is a psychiatrist, which means he can prescribe medication, which I can't do. I'm a psychologist. But I'll tell you what I think, Larissa. The symptoms you've been experiencing for the past five years are typical of depressive patients, and I agree with Dr. Chakraborty that you are experiencing a depression."

I cry.

"Now," he continues, "people with depression have symptoms that people with schizophrenia experience. The symptoms overlap. That's why Dr. Chakraborty thinks that you're schizophrenic. A lot of the symptoms you have from the depression also happen to be symptoms of schizophrenia... But people with schizophrenia have an altered perception of reality. One of my friends, for instance... I'm treating him right now. He believes that aliens are trying to get in touch with him through the things he hears on the radio."

He gets a faraway look on his face as if he's thinking of his friend.

"So he has an altered perception of reality. I don't sense that with you. You seem very lucid to me."

"So you don't think I'm schizophrenic. But Dr. Chakraborty does. Who am I supposed to believe? And maybe you're wrong about me having depression. If he can be wrong, you can be too. Maybe I have nothing."

Daniel smiles a little, but then quickly suppresses it.

"Well, you and I are going to do some tests together, okay, Larissa? I'm going to be running these tests in order to find a diagnosis."

"Thank God!" I exclaim.

He looks surprised. "How so?"

"Well, Dr. Chakraborty diagnosed me yesterday just by talking to me for like five minutes. At least you're going to do some actual stuff and you know, do it properly."

"Right. So you're going to be seeing me for the next few days, and in your spare time I'd like you to fill out some questionnaires for me," he says, shuffling the papers on his clipboard. "Do you think you can do that?"

I nod.

Daniel smiles approvingly. With every passing moment, I like this guy more and more.

"Good. I'll give you the questionnaire right now. I'd like for you to fill it out within the next two days. You can work on it during your spare time and during schoolroom time. Sound good? Yes? Good. Now, I want you to do something for me. Could you please tell me, in your own words, what you think caused the depression? I'd like to hear it, please."

Daniel picks up his clipboard and holds a pen ready over it, then looks up at me expectantly, waiting for me to begin.

"I don't know where to start," I say.

"Start at the beginning," is his response. "That's a very good place to start. Tell me absolutely everything you can think of that can help me to help you."

"There's not really anything you can do to help me," I say. "I hate to tell you this, but there's nothing you can do. There's nothing anyone can do. I don't know why you think you can make a difference. This isn't something you're going to cure. Trust me, Daniel, I've tried everything. And I think I know myself better than you do."

"Well, Larissa," says Daniel in a way that makes me think he must have some kind of unshaskeable core of peace within him. Otherwise how could he possibly be so soothing?

"I don't doubt that you know yourself better than anyone. But we're going to try some things you haven't tried before to make this better for you. Until you try it, you won't know if it will work. I can help you, Larissa, but only if you're willing to try."

Daniel looks at me as if he would be very disappointed if I didn't.

It's the word "try" that gets to me. I've never been afraid to at least try something.

I try to begin.

"On the whole, I'm just exhausted," I say hesitantly. "I've tried everything already. I told you. This has been happening for over the past five years. You're not just going to make things better overnight."

"No, you're right, Larissa," Daniel says soothingly. "That's going to take some time. But I think you can do it; you're a smart girl."

"Yeah, I guess, but I don't think you know what you're up against."

"I've been practising psychology for many years, Larissa. I've seen many patients. I know what this thing is. I can help you."

"Have you helped them?"

"Yes."

"How long have you been practising psychology?"

"For about six years now." He smiles.

"How old are you?"

"Thirty-six." He doesn't look thirty-six.

"Wow, you're young to be a doctor," I say, smiling in spite of myself.

"Thank you," he says humbly, and I like him a little. I like all humble people.

"Where did you go to study?"

"I went to New York University to study psychology."

"I've heard of that place!" I say excitedly.

"Have you?"

"Yes. It's quite famous."

"Yes, it is."

Daniel smiles.

"You must have taken a long time to become a psychologist."

"About six years."

"Did you always know you wanted to be a psychologist?"

"No. I wanted to be a lawyer at first."

"That's what I want to be!"

"Do you? Why?" He looks genuinely interested.

"Because it looks cool... Like, I only know about lawyers from what I've seen in movies, and I know it's not usually like that, but I like that they try to do the right thing and protect people and help people, and it's just so cool."

He smiles again.

"Well, Larissa," he says, shifting his weight on the chair, "I wouldn't put it past you to achieve your goals."

I stare at him in amazement. Does he really believe that?

"Now, are you ready to tell me what you think caused the depression? I want you to try thinking about it and tell me what happened, so I can help you and maybe later you won't feel confused when you think about it, all right?"

Daniel really wants to help me. I can tell. Nobody has actually been interested in hearing my sob stories before. My family knows most of them, having watched me go through them. It's different, though, with this stranger. He doesn't know me, why does he want to help me? Normally, I realize, I'd feel suspicious of him. Somehow he doesn't have that effect on me, though.

"Well," I say after thinking for a moment, "There's nothing really to tell. You know, that's what's strange. People think that something happened. But nothing happened to me. I didn't, like, get raped, or beaten, I didn't do drugs or have sex, nobody I love died, no guy dumped me... I just was depressed. That's all there is to it."

Daniel sits looking at me, writing things down. I start to feel the anxiety returning and my head getting fuzzy.

"I won't ever know what made me suddenly feel out of whack, like you know nothing would be okay, like I was a hopeless, useless person who couldn't think straight and couldn't make simple decisions. Like there was no point in living. That's all in the past now. But I can't find the solution to fixing what went wrong."

"When did you first start feeling symptoms?"

"Eleven years old."

I stare at the bookshelf I could see above his shoulder, looking at the titles about positive psychology and child psychology, adolescent problem behavior and stress. I wonder how horrible it is to see children with problems all the time, every day, so unhappy and traumatized. How depressing it must be.

After a few long moments, I realize that he hasn't said anything since I answered his question, and I've been staring at the bookshelf, thinking, in silence.

I glance at Daniel.

His brow is furrowed. I look away so he can't tell what I'm thinking.

"Can you look at me please?" he says.

I do.

"Why don't you look at me when you're talking to me?" he asks.

"Um."

The silence stretches on.

"When you don't look at me, I wonder if you just aren't feeling confident enough."

He stops and pauses, and I realize it's my turn to speak.

"I don't have any confidence," I say, sighing a long, deep, tremulous sigh. "How can I, when I'm so unable to live every day like normal people do? Normal people wake up and get up from bed. They aren't afraid to walk out the front door. They go to school, work, and to do things any normal person is capable of doing. This is what normal people do: They survive. But for me, even going from one minute to another takes such an effort. I just can't seem to move forward. I'm stuck in the past. I'm trying to figure out what happened to me. I feel like, if I figure out what happened, what made me depressed, I can undo it. Or, at the very least, avoid what makes me depressed."

"Let's back up. You were eleven years old?"

"Yeah…" I decide to talk about it, just because I'm so sick of thinking of it all by myself.

"I was very tired and slept all the time. I was also fighting a lot with my mother, who was pregnant with Elizabeth. It was a few months before I got my period for the first time. I was terribly hormonal. My mom was just as hormonal from her pregnancy. We clashed all the time. She was always yelling at me for some reason. You know, nagging me, screaming, having fits over nothing... I can't talk to her without getting her mad. I started, like, hibernating. I couldn't concentrate in school because I wanted to sleep all the time. My grades went down because I wouldn't do my homework; I'd just come home and fall asleep until dinner, wake up, eat dinner, and then go back to sleep and wake up the next morning. I walked around like I was a zombie. I didn't see anything, couldn't feel anything, and I didn't want to talk to anybody or do anything with anyone. I cried for no reason. I felt so anxious and so scared. I didn't like to do the things I liked to do anymore, like read or write, listen to music or watch movies. I just wanted to sleep for as long as I could and never wake up."

"Have you ever heard or seen things that are not actually there?"

"Yes. I did hear voices one night in May... 2001. Yes, May 2001. They were just talking and then they started to scream at me, and I couldn't hear what they were saying but I knew they were mad at me and wanted me to be scared."

"How many times?"

"Um, five times, I think, in 2001. A couple of times when I was fourteen. And then the other night, after taking the medication Dr. Chakraborty prescribed."

He scribbles furiously on the paper on his clip-board.

"What else can you tell me?"

"When I was twelve, things started to get better. When I was thirteen, I was acting normal but I felt even worse. It was a terrible feeling. My head was so confused. You have no idea. It was so strange. I tried to act fine, but I knew things were not okay. I still didn't feel good about doing things that I used to do before."

"Like what?"

"When I read books, I couldn't understand what I was reading, or comprehend... like, I can't really describe it. It was like such a waste of time, reading something, like a full page or even a sentence, and then stopping to think and realizing you have no idea what you've just read. It's like how you feel after you haven't slept in a few days... exhausted. It was so exhausting to read just a few sentences. Going to school felt like such a chore. It still does, actually, but twenty times worse... I was angry all the time. I stopped playing with my siblings, talking to people, and I was in a bubble because everything was so confusing and overwhelming..."

I am getting riled up as I think about it and say it out loud. I remember, as I talk, what it felt like, and I begin to cry.

I can't put into words what it felt like. The feelings are beyond what words can express.

Daniel stops writing and just looks at me, waiting, I suppose, for me to stop my crying.

"I don't know why," I say finally, after gulping a few times, "Why when I talk about it, it doesn't seem so bad, but I'm telling you... it *was*, it really was."

"I believe you, Larissa," Daniel says quietly. "I don't think it wasn't that bad at all."

"But when I talk about it, I feel like telling myself, 'What is wrong with you? Why did you do that? Why don't you just get over it, stop sleeping so much, and just... you know... wake up, get over it, get better and just stop this craziness?' "

I sob for a while. When I stop and look at Daniel between wiping my eyes on my sleeve, he looks thoughtful.

"Larissa, you can't possibly tell yourself to get over it just like that, my friend."

"My friend"? Since when did I become his *friend*? I find myself give a little smile.

Daniel smiles back. To be on the receiving end of his kind smile in the midst of all this confusion and anger is like receiving an unexpected cold sundae on a sweltering July afternoon, when the sun is at its hottest and the air seems thick with heat.

It's like being told you're beautiful on a day when you feel like utter shit.

CHAPTER 5

LET IT BE NORMAL

I can't sleep well. Each night, the nurses go to each room during their rounds and shine a flashlight into each patient's face to see if they're asleep. But in doing so, they wake the patients up. At least, they wake me up every hour when they do this.

At around six one morning, an extremely obese nurse comes into the room. She explains that she is going to draw my blood for a blood test.

"In three hours," she says, "they're going to send you to get an MRI and CAT scan done."

She has trouble finding the vein to poke through with the needle, and ends up poking me a few times in order to find it. I watch her and the sun starting to come up and shine through the slits in the curtains, and listen to her labored breathing.

When she's done, she leaves and I fall into sleep, only to be awakened again by the same nurse, who directs me to a wheelchair.

It's strange to be wheeled around the hospital in a wheelchair when I'm fully capable of using my legs. Two hospital volunteers take me to another floor. All the stares I'm receiving make me feel kind of like an alien from another galaxy. I know I look disoriented. My hair is sticking up all over the place, and my face is all tired.

An old lady gives me a hospital gown to wear and a bag to put my clothes in. I change into the hospital gown and wait. Finally she takes me into a room where I sit on a chair in front of her. She puts some kind of jelly on specific areas of my scalp and attaches wires to my scalp where the jelly is.

"How old are you? What school do you go to?" she asks as she works over me. "Do you have siblings?"

"Sixteen. St. Marcellinus. Yes, four siblings."

"How old are they?"

"Fourteen, twelve, nine, five."

"They must look up to you! Their big sister," she says.

"Yeah. I guess."

"Are they a handful?"

"Not really."

"Isn't that adorable! You have a nice big family,

Larissa."

"Thanks."

I pray with my eyes shut tightly as she looks at the computer screen, examining what I suppose are pictures of my brain. I feel anxiety rising in my chest. *Please. Let it be normal, God.* And then I add, against my better judgment: *Unless you don't want it to be normal, God, then please let it be abnormal.*

The lady takes off her gloves.

"Okay, Larissa," she says in a bright voice. "I don't see anything out of the ordinary here. Take care, Larissa... All the very best."

Two different high school volunteers come for me and wheel me into a room with a large machine. I lie on the cold hard bed of the machine, and a nurse comes in and injects my left arm with a huge needle, which makes me flinch.

"This will change the colour of your blood so the machine can read it," she says and disappears.

After about ten minutes, the bed moves me until my head and shoulders are under a dome-like scanner. The needle doesn't hurt. The machine starts up. It whirs and makes grinding and chugging sounds. I try to hum a little song in my head. A conglomeration of "Summer of 69" and "Hips Don't Lie" works its way into my mind and plays over and over again.

I am too tired to keep track of the exact lyrics, however. What seems like a million thoughts are buzzing around at the same time inside my mind, so instead I try to think of other things: My father and mother. My siblings: Rachelle, Stephanie, Mathias and Elizabeth. The hallways of St. Marcellinus and the students in red sweaters crowding around, squeezing past each other, trying to get to their next classes. I hear in my mind the voices of some of those students, greeting me and saying good morning or see you tomorrow. The feel of piano keys under my fingers. Grandma's laugh. The smell of my father's cooking.

I think of my wedding, the one I'll have when I'm in my late twenties, probably. I know who I want to be at my wedding, what flowers will decorate the pews, the bouquet I'll have in my hands, and the songs we'll play. Everything is decided in my mind, except the identity of the man who will stand next to me at the front and say, "I do."

Please let my future husband not mind that I'm mentally ill, God. Please free him from any misconceptions or discrimination against me and against those who are like me.

The nurse comes and takes the needle out. Then she grasps me under my arm, helps me sit up and guides me to the wheelchair and wheels me to the waiting room.

In the waiting room, I hear James Blunt's voice singing, "You're beautiful, you're beautiful, it's true."

I pretend James Blunt is singing the song for me, that James Blunt thinks I'm beautiful. It just reminds me again that I probably look like a handful of crap, sitting here, rumpled, in a hospital gown with the jelly in my hair and my unhappy eyes staring out without any life in them. I try to rake my fingers through my hair and comb out the knots. It doesn't work.

As I sit and wait for the next volunteer to come and collect me and bring me back to that depressing adolescent mental health unit in the basement, I think about everything that has gone through my mind during the MRI and CAT scans.

I'm looking forward to things like going home, like seeing my siblings, like getting married. I just realize this: the thought of living a normal life still appeals to me.

Until now, I'd never understood the implications of this—that I want to *live*.

CHAPTER 6

BECOMING SILVER GIRL

"Wakey, wakey, Larissa!" says a singsong voice.

It appears to be a pirate! I emerge from beneath the blanket to peek at it. Even without my glasses, which are perched on the wooden dresser next to my hospital bed, I can make out one heavily made-up eye, the other covered by a black patch, a gold tooth, a bright red polka-dot bandana and cropped white-blond hair. The hair tells me that this pirate is Janice, the recreational therapist.

"Did you have a good sleep last night?" asks Janice.

I pull the covers over my head. When I'm underneath the covers, I can pretend that it's still night, and that I don't have to face yet another day on this stupid mental health unit.

"I don't know. Why are you dressed like a pirate?"

"Well, what day is it?"

I take a guess. "Halloween?" I realize now that it must be: it's the end of October.

"Exactly. We're going out tonight to trick-or-treat!"

❊   ❊   ❊

We go out dressed in our normal clothes: jeans, t-shirts and hoodies.

I feel queasy as we go from house to house. I remember my face in the mirror back in the hospital and how awful it looked. I feel torn between wanting to go back and hide, and wanting never to go back to that hospital ever again. Not back to where it's confirmed that I am, in fact, crazy. Being in there only makes me crazier, I'm sure of it.

I grasp at things to make myself feel better: The smell of the grass? The feel of the wind against my face? The memory of trick-or-treating as a child with my parents and with my siblings, dressed up in the costumes Mama created with her sewing machine?

After half an hour, I've collected a fair amount of chocolates and candies and a random can of Coke. We approach a lit home with a scarecrow hanging by the mailbox. About seven twenty-somethings stand in a circle next to the car parked in the driveway, drinking from beer bottles. They turn and watch us approach.

"Aren't you a little too old to be trick-or-treating?" one of the men calls to us. "Trying to take the candies we've got specially for the little ones, eh?"

I'm afraid that someone will answer him. No one does. We walk past them to the porch and to the front door. The twelve-year-old patient, Jason, rings a few times. When no one answers after the third ring, we turn to leave, but the man who spoke earlier puts down his beer bottle.

"Is no one coming?"

"No," answers Jason. The man comes up to the front door, opens it, and suddenly, the smell of fresh flowers comes wafting through that front door.

I think of my mother and her own flowers, the flowers she slaves away at, arranging through the night in order to make it in time for the couple who have ordered them for their wedding the next day. Even more unexpected, though, is the sound of a piano flowing from somewhere inside the house. It gives my heart a twist, unfurls it and leaves it feeling wrung out and tired of fighting.

The man reappears with a basket of candy and starts to hand out chocolate bars as the piano starts to play one of my favourite songs.

"Sail on, Silver Girl, sail on by..." He's singing under his breath in time with the piano. "Your time has come to shine, all your dreams are on their way... You're doing great, Dora!" he shouts.

The piano stops.

"Thanks, Tony," says a little girl's voice. Then the piano starts up once more.

He glances around at us in disapproval.

"Why do you guys go trick-or-treating? Don't you have better things to do than take chocolate and candy meant for kids?" he says. "Look, you're not even dressed up! If you're going to go trick-or-treating at your age, you might as well make an effort to dress up."

I feel myself crack a little inside. It's the exact same thing I think of when I see teenagers without costumes at my own door.

Everyone accepts his chocolate bars and leaves until finally I'm the only one on the porch. I stand in front of the man, holding out my limp, half-empty Longo's plastic bag, feeling small, pathetic and stupid. I stare at this stranger before me, at his ruffled hair and bloodshot eyes, feeling more connected to him in this moment than I have with the other patients in two weeks, because he knows what it's like to feel robbed by teenagers on Halloween night, and he's doing what I'd be doing if I were home right now.

He tosses the candy from where he stands at the door but it misses my plastic bag.

"Whoops!" he says in a loud voice. I bend down, pick it up and toss it in my bag. Then I glance back and say, "Thank you," before I turn to leave.

I love being one of those people who says thank you on Halloween.

"You dropped something," the man says and points. "It fell off your wrist."

Before I can do anything, he bends down and picks up the plastic hospital wristband that the nurses put on me when I was admitted. It says my name, the hospital's name, my birth date, and that I'm allergic to penicillin.

I see his face change.

"Here you go!" he says in a happy voice. I hold out my palm but he slips the wristband over it. "There! Here—here's more just for you!"

He vigorously grabs a handful of candy out of his basket and drops it into my bag.

"Have a nice night, sweetheart!" His bloodshot eyes stare at me, round and bulging.

"Thanks. You too." I'm surprised at how normal my voice sounds.

I walk down the porch, past his beer-drinking friends and towards my group, which has already moved two houses ahead of me, so I run to catch up with them. A tall boy is lagging behind. I've seen him before and heard the other patients call him Jake.

"Hey, Jake," I say to him.

He glances over at me.

"I wish I was at home," he says after a moment. "I wish I was trick-or-treating with my buds, or at least, not in that shithole."

"I feel the same way," I say. "I wish I was Silver Girl, sailing on by, with a friend right behind me, waiting to lay his or her life down for me."

He looks down at me without moving his head.

"You're weird," he says.

"I know," I say. I can tell from the look on his face that he's confused about what I said about being Silver Girl, but all the same, I feel like I've made a friend.

Janice waves furiously from down the block. We jog towards her, swinging our plastic Longo's bags in our hands, and when we catch up, we open the Coke cans that we got from an old lady a few houses back, and drink to getting out of the hospital.

"Yo, what did that guy say to you?" Jake asks me.

"Oh. You know, he didn't really say much with words. He said a lot more things with his eyes. He looked really sad when he realized I was from the hospital."

"Stupid drunkard," says Jake. "We don't need his goddamn sympathy."

"I wish I were back there, smelling the sweet smell of flowers from inside where it's warm and listening to the piano," I say. "I love that song, 'Bridge Over Troubled Water'."

"Oh, lovely song," says Janice.

"I think I was meant to hear that song tonight," I say.

"What do you mean?" Janice asks sharply.

"I feel that God played that song for me because he knows I love that song and that I would feel hopeful if I were to hear it. So He played it for me tonight, because I was losing hope."

"Losing hope?" Janice looks at me like I'm about to slit my wrists in front of her. "What do you mean?"

I'm about to speak, but Jake interrupts.

"That's crazy talk," he says. "You're schizophrenic, aren't you?"

"That's none of your business, Jake," says Janice before I can answer. "We ought to be heading back to the hospital, guys. It's getting late."

As we walk back to the hospital, I pretend I am Silver Girl and all my dreams are on their way.

For some reason, it doesn't seem impossible.

CHAPTER 7

HOMECOMING

There are no enormous, heartfelt goodbyes exchanged with any other patients or the nurses when I leave the hospital, alone, overwhelmingly relieved that I am finally on my way home.

I leave quietly.

It's early afternoon when I am officially discharged. The papers are prepared. The sour-faced red-haired nurse whose name I don't know opens her arms when she sees me walking to the front door. She wants me to hug her. I do, surprised, and feel a smacking kiss on my forehead.

I leave my fear about going to St. Marcellinus Secondary School at the mental health unit. I leave these fears behind. For good.

I grab my coat, take one last look around at

the nursing station, the dining area, and the living room, and walk out the door. A fear like that has no place in my life.

I am determined, when I leave, to return to high school after this brief stint in the unit.

Although my stay in the unit has been short, I feel it has transformed me in some way. I am not who I was before.

I don't realize that I've spent four weeks as an inpatient and two weeks as an outpatient in the unit until I count the weeks that have gone by, standing outside the main entrance of the hospital, looking for the taxi designated to bring me home.

It's been six weeks? I was in there for six weeks? It wasn't long at all. It felt like forever, though.

I am scared that today I leave the unit for good. I don't feel everything inside me is right. Don't think that it's going to feel right ever again, I say to myself. That is the surest way to fall into the same hole again.

It was not the terrifying experience I thought it would be. I feel almost like myself again, not quite right, but I'm not as bad as before.

Seriously? It's been six weeks?

I watch people flit in and out of the main doors of the hospital, some being pushed in their wheelchairs. An unwanted memory rises: that of myself being pushed in a wheelchair by a volunteer, my hair unkempt and wild, my eyes out of focus and my face betraying that I feel as if I've been derailed from my tracks, on my way to get an MRI and a CAT scan done.

It's about three in the afternoon but the wintry sky is already darkening and everyone seems to be in a hurry to get home because rain is coming. What a relief to not have to come back here, to where everyone is either ill or getting ill or finding out if they're ill or in relations with someone who is.

The hospital stint is over. What a relief. Six weeks. I leave knowing that it could have been worse. It could have been longer. They could have said they were diagnosing me as officially schizophrenic. I could be on a dozen weird-named medications. I could be on medications that are not working. I could be hearing voices all day that tell me to hurt other people or myself. I could just be inert. I could still be wallowing in despair, not willing to return to high school. I could be one of those people who don't get visitors for whatever reason when they're in hospital. I just could be a million other things that would certainly have led to a longer hospitalization. I could have never gone to the hospital, never gotten the treatment I needed. The hospital stint is over. And the way it could have been, never was.

Thank God.

I see a taxi driver waving at me through the rain

a couple of hours after the time the nurse on duty today told me the taxi company said he'd be here. I arrive at the taxi a couple of seconds later, splashing in my boots, diving into the back seat amid the chaos of taxi cabs and other cars either picking up or dropping people off at the entrance.

I leave.

I leave the hospital with a certain confidence in myself, that I, Mei-Hui Larissa, survived the stint in the hospital. I feel good. I feel what seems to be a shadow of a feeling of accomplishment, that I got through this, and I am better for it.

As the taxi carries me back to my home in Mississauga, I have the distinct feeling of being watched by everyone else driving on the road alongside our cab. Everyone is watching me.

No. Stop. Stop now. It's over. You're done with those thoughts.

Yes, it could have been worse. It could be that those thoughts are my unshakeable reality. And yet they're not. By some grace of God, I know these thoughts are not true, not real, and won't help me. They are to be banished from my mind for good. They're useless. Throw them out.

By the grace of God, what could have been my life, my reality, my struggle, was not. It didn't happen that way.

Imagine being someone with a mental illness,

someone who goes to places in her mind that no one can guess or fathom or has ever been to before. I glimpsed some of that while living in the mental health unit at William Osler. I saw the way the patients' eyes glazed over. I would sometimes disappear from myself at any given time when something—a comment or a thought—would trigger an unwanted feeling or memory, and I know that living with an unhealthy mind is a terrifying existence, one that I wouldn't wish on anybody.

As the taxi takes us on the highway towards home, I wonder, *What am I going to do now?*

* * *

I'm home.

I walk around in my bare feet after taking off my coat and hanging it up on the closet. I look at the kitchen, at the dishes piled in the sink, waiting to be loaded into the dishwasher, at the bright yellow-painted walls and toys on the floor, our DVD set, and the unmade beds in the bedrooms. I lie down on the bed I share with Rachelle and sigh. I think about Daniel and what he said about my academic test scores, especially the reading comprehension score: "Take this and run with it."

What exactly did he mean by that? I should have asked when I had the chance.

I get up from bed and turn on the CD player. The middle chorus of Bon Jovi's "Livin' on Prayer" blasts through the silence.

"Take my hand and we'll make it, I swear... Whoah! Livin' on a prayer... Whoahhhh, we're half-way there..."

I start jumping around as if I'm Jon Bon Jovi himself, playing on an imaginary guitar, strumming the air and rocking my body. I can't move around well in these jeans so I strip them off and take off my bulky sweater and shirt.

There. That's it. I can definitely move in this bra and underwear.

"WHOAHHH, WE'RE HALWAY THERE! WHOAH, LIVIN' ON A PRAYER! OH, LIVIN' ON A PRAYER!"

I scream the "whoah" and yell the "oh". And I jump on the "livin' on a prayer", my eyes closed, my body bent over my non-existent guitar, my hair wet from sweat. The bed flops up and down as I jump, and the frame makes a rattling sound.

During the tenth "Take my hand, we'll make it I swear," I catch, in the corner of my eye, through the window, the man from the house behind us, looking up at me from his lawn. He's always outside, walk-ing around his garden with his dog and admiring his flowers. Usually it's me who takes notice of him without his knowledge.

Today, it's the other way round.

I slam myself down on the bed, facedown, glance at the clock, and realize I've been dancing around in my underwear for the past hour and a half, listening to "Livin' on a Prayer" on repeat and pretending I am Jon Bon Jovi.

And Tim, the Neigbour to the South, has seen me. And watched me. For how long? Oh, my God… Hopefully he's not a creeper or an ass.

I duck low as I make my way to the washroom so he doesn't see me through the window and grab my clothes and run into the shower.

After my shower, I slip downstairs to the kitchen and munch on some chocolate until I hear the front door opening and my siblings swarm in and find me.

I'm home.

They wash their hands. Then Mama comes into the kitchen and starts to cook some linguini for dinner.

We watch *House* on TV while eating our linguini. We watch episode after episode until four in the morning.

I'm home.

CHAPTER 8

LIVING WITH
IMPOSSIBILITIES

In February, I return to school to start my second
semester at St. Marcellinus.

I write a letter to Daniel. I won't ever see him
again. But I want to thank him.

I say:

Happy Chinese New Year, Daniel, and thank you for
taking care of me while I was in the hospital. Do you remem-
ber the poem I wrote while I was in the hospital last October?
I ask him. The one for the Remembrance Day contest at the
Canadian Legion? Well, I won. First place. And it went on
to the next round in the competition and won second there.

The final poem goes like this:

Becoming Silver Girl

Lieutenant Colonel Powell knew just what he'd say
When the men came together to pray that day
So beautiful, blue, warm, and clear
It had been chosen to remember those they'd held dear
They were now weathered, frail, and grey
But never would they forget the men who lay
Now dead in Flanders Fields.

They'd gathered here many years ago
Assembled in uniform, they stood row by row,
Some wanted peace—others wanted more
More freedom, more independence, and more choice
They were willing to fight if it gave them a voice.
The boys felt lonely, anxious, and tired
And it felt worse with every shot fired.

The old men remembered when the colonel once said:
"We're going to do our job and get out fast;
I promise you when we leave, I'll be last.
So hold tight, boys—or should I say men—
It won't be long till this war is at its end.
Soon you'll be home, you'll be with her.
Nothing lasts forever, that's for sure."

So in the end, both sides lost
The reasons I went were not worth the cost.
Today we have families; some others do not
We are alive, though we all fought.
We've tried to tell the world, war is in vain
I know for sure in my heart, it has no gain
We tell them, when all is said and done,

We have all been beaten, no side has won.
Have we done our job? Is the future secure?
Some things may last forever, can peace be for sure?

I enclose it in the Chinese New Year card and then I send it off to him at the hospital.

❅   ❅   ❅

"**S**tory! Story! Story!"
        Mathias is begging for a story again.

At night, on the bunk bed, I start a story and my brother finishes it. It's our nightly ritual.

"'Robin entered his room'… Now you finish it."

Sometimes at night, I wake up and listen for screaming voices and footsteps around the bunk-bed, but there's no sign of them.

I can't hear anything but my brother's small breaths into his pillow.

One night, I have a dream that I'm at the park near my house, standing at the bottom of a slide. Next to me is Daniel… He wants me to walk up the slide. *It's too hard*, I tell him, *I'll just slide back down.* And then I walk away and the dream ends.

I think about that dream sometimes. Daniel asked me to do the impossible—he asked me to get better and I wouldn't even give it a try because after getting better, I figure I could just fall back down again. I wouldn't try to get better because of that. I wouldn't try because if I were to fall back down, my efforts to get better will have been in vain.

I wouldn't even try in a dream.

It shames me. I feel myself wrapped in my shame and in my self-pity as if in a cocoon. A self-pity party is a terrible thing. Add shame, and you've now got a concoction of fiery resistance to getting well, re-covering completely, and going on your merry way. I see what I'm doing to myself by bringing in the hazardous self-pity and I see it take me down, lower and lower into desolation.

Try to live your life without the self-pity, and take the responsibility and the blame!

It's hard to go on your merry way after you've just been derailed from normal life.

After you've just been derailed? Or after you have derailed your own life?

As I listen to myself think at night, as I try to fall asleep, I realize how much I'm pinning this dark point in my life on something, someone, outside of myself, and I have to remind myself that this is *my* fault.

Not anyone else's.

Don't blame anyone else for it, I say to myself sternly.

I listen to myself say it but I don't internalize it. I don't believe it. I want someone to blame for this disaster, for this suffering. I want to be able to point my finger and say, "You did this!" and be able to ask that person, "Why? Why me?"

Just why I want to do this I don't really know. All I know is I'm listening to myself talk and trying to rework the way I frame the situation, so that I understand internally that this is happening because of what I did, of my failure to get better, be normal, live a decent life, be motivated, think clearly.

I listen to my own voice reasoning and try to believe it above the automatic and hurtful words in my head.

I listen, waiting for the self-pity to cease.

It doesn't work. I listen to myself in vain. *What is wrong with me?*

I try to fight myself, with the words I use, with the way I see the world.

It's never going to change. It's never going to get better. I may as well give up.

Give yourself love. Not pity. Self-love. No self-pity. Love. Love will save the day.

No... Give up. Don't even bother.

Try. Just try. Live with the impossibility of walking up a slide in the park. Maybe that impossibility is possible to live with.

I argue with myself and contradict myself until I fall asleep each night, thinking of the new day about to arrive, and try to be grateful and excited.

Come back. I try to coax my true self out of hiding.

Come back and do it right *this time.*

* * *

"Give me some guidance, God." I stare up at the ceiling. "Guidance, please, God."

I say it when I wake up every morning, before I even raise my back from the surface of the bed.

Mathias snores in the bed below me. I mutter incessantly: "Guidance, God. I depend on some guidance, please."

I listen.

I listen in vain.

"Show me what you want me to do, God."

Now and then I remember to thank God when I wake up. But usually I don't. I'm always requesting guidance, help, healing. Anything that God can give me.

"Wake up!" my mother yells from the top of the stairs leading to the basement.

"Coming!"

It's my responsibility to make my brother get up in the mornings or we'll be late for school. I feel in the darkness for his face. I massage his hair.

"Wake up, brother dear..."

It takes us half an hour to emerge from the basement, with him leaning on me, his eyes still closed, snoring. I support his weight with my body and pull him up the second flight of stairs to the upstairs bedrooms where our sisters are brushing their teeth in the bathroom and changing from their pajamas into school attire.

"No, no, no! I don't want to go to school!" he says.

"Neither do I, but I'm going to go," I say to him firmly.

The medication isn't working. I find it hard to concentrate in class. I wander from thought to thought aimlessly throughout the day. I can't keep up in classes. I think of the people in the hospital. I wonder what everything is for. I see no point in anything.

I only want to go home and sleep.

I don't, though. I force myself to stay in the classes that are not making any sense to me, the biology and chemistry, history and philosophy.

Somehow, I feel a little worse than before I went to the hospital... Although I'm functioning, I'm functioning kind of as a dead person would, devoid of emotion, having no interest in or feeling for each day. I don't tell this to anybody because I don't want to end up in the hospital again.

I am scared that if I do, the doctors won't let me out like they did the last time.

EPILOGUE
DEGREES OF SANITY

I guess you could say nothing scares me anymore. When you've had an experience where you understand so deeply in your core that we are all interconnected—by our sameness, that is, by our ability to draw on sanity until there's no sanity left to be had—you start to realize that there's not much separating each of the people here on earth but varying degrees of craziness. Of all the people we could have been and dreamed we'd someday be, we never thought we'd arrive at this level of insanity, whatever the words "level of insanity" mean to you, or in this state of being. It does mean different things for different people. For some, whoever goes back to a man who beats her every day and can't get over his alcohol abuse must be insane. For others, the mad are those who drive their kids to school every morning after making their breakfast and ensure their own presence at the front of the school, waiting for their kids to appear, when the school bell rings to signal the end of the day.

I won't begin to try to list the number of things that can be classified as insanity in this world. In the deep recesses of our hearts, there are plenty of things people do that we secretly believe are downright crazy whether or not anyone else thinks so.

Or you may think all of it is crazy, and that you are the only sane one in the world.

I do know the deviant and sometimes dark ways in which the state of my mind, healthy or unhealthy at any given moment, gives itself away, reveals itself to be deviant. Or reveals itself to be wonderful and healthy, reacting in normal ways and thinking normal thoughts. I can also tell you that I never thought I'd reach that level of derangement and absurdity, a delusional and strange way of thinking.

I ask myself every day, what's the point? What is the reason for all this suffering?

Well, you may say, of course, it's only a crazy person who looks for reason in something like this, where there is none to be found...

Or you may think it's perfectly normal to want some validation and confirmation that what you've suffered means *something*.

Who wouldn't want there to be a meaning, a purpose for their despair, to be reassured that the suffering they bore was not for nothing, did not go to waste, shouldn't have happened, or worse, did not really happen, and was all in their head?

And I can assure you that it doesn't matter, in the end, whether it happened or whether you think it's normal or crazy to wonder if it had a purpose.

Everyone's capable of the utmost cruelty and everyone's capable of unexpected kindness. The in-between is what counts, really—how we get each other from here to there, from here to insanity, how we keep each other here rather than there, there where we are all capable of doing and thinking outrageous things we never believed we could do or think, some harmful, some beautiful. I believe it's an obligation that we all have towards each other, to keep those we know and we love, and even those we don't, from going over to abandonment of reason.

It's a paradox that even the abandonment of reason has reason in it, although I'm not totally interested in that. I just want to know about the in-between. The things we do every day add up to the despair that results in the crossing over of one from here to the other side where sanity is gone. And sometimes the things we do leave us utterly content, thoroughly warm and comfortable, and despair, no matter how many times it strikes, doesn't avail in dragging someone over to insanity, because no matter how many times you've stood at the brink of despair, you've never really lost until you decide to go over.

We're everyone else's keepers. We're ultimately responsible for everyone else we are in contact with. I guess if more people knew this, they would listen more when they heard someone speak, they would see, truly see, with their hearts and think with concern and compassion rather than judging. Because one person over the brink of despair and into insanity is one person too many.

And once you lose your mind, it's hard to get it back. And even if you get it back, it's hard to mend. And if you do mend it, it's likely to get lost or broken again... and mending it doesn't make it whole, but "just usable."

Living with a "just usable" mind can be done, but that doesn't mean it's acceptable...

There are plenty of us walking around with minds that are just barely usable, that have been broken or lost or mended, or all three, and I am one of them.

You don't have to be one of the walking wounded to recognize that insanity can strike anyone, anywhere, at any time, whatever the circumstances.

It doesn't scare me, though. Because in spite of all this chaos and the lack of love in the world, I feel that I now know the common thing that unites us all beyond all the usual things they always say make us alike: that we all are on a harrowing journey towards collectively shouldering each other's weight to keep each of us sane and healthy, away from the vortex of despair, away from the insanity.

ACKNOWLEDGEMENTS

Thank you to Lin and Frederick Ho, my parents, who played with me, fought for me, taught and encouraged and loved me, and who always save me every time I've had a fall.

Thank you also to my dearest and most beloved siblings, Rachelle, Stephanie, Mathias and Elizabeth. We share so much: our parents, specific dreams, favourite songs, old memories, inside jokes, and whatever else there may be. Thank you always for your tenacious support and love.

Thank you to my grandma, Theresa Choo, who is always there on the best and worst of days.

Thank you to Alan Lovette, who assumed the role of cheerleader in my life without being asked to and who is cut from the same cloth as I am. Without you I would not have gotten this book done or realized I am capable of not only surviving, but living, life.

Thank you to Amir Ahmed and Luke Sawczak, who read these stories before anyone else and saw the goodness in them before I did.

Thank you to Guy Allen, who has never hesitated to provide reassurance whenever I need to hear that I'm good enough to write. Your wonderful strength lays itself down like a bridge over troubled water so I can cross over.

ABOUT THE AUTHOR

Larissa Fleurette Ho believes that writing is a calling, not a job. Her credits include having been the editor-in-chief of the student creative nonfiction anthology *Mindwaves*. Her story "Not Still Me", featured in this collection, won the 2014  Mississauga Arts Council (MARTYs) Emerging Literary Artist Award. She is on the brink of graduating from the University of Toronto Mississauga and will go on to complete an MFA in Creative Writing at the University of British Columbia—after which she will travel the world. She enjoys storytelling more than anything else in life and spending time with family and friends.

Made in the USA
Charleston, SC
11 January 2016